A long time ago, a giant lived in a castle. The castle had a big garden. There were lots of beautiful trees and flowers in the garden.

Some children lived near the castle. They liked the Giant's garden, but the Giant did not like people. 'You can't play here! It's *my* garden!' he shouted. The Giant was selfish.

selfish

1

One day, the Giant went to visit his brother. 'The Giant's going to be away for a long time,' said the children. 'Now we can play in his garden.' They were very happy.

Every day they went to the beautiful garden and played. They climbed the trees. They swam in the river. They ran on the grass. They chased butterflies.

The children liked the garden in all the seasons of the year.

In the spring the flowers and leaves grew.

In the summer the children rolled on the green grass.

In the autumn the leaves were orange and red. They fell from the trees and the children played with them.

In the winter the children played in the snow. They made snowmen.

Different children came to the garden every year.

snow   snowmen

 **Puzzles**

1. What are the seasons? Write the right words.

IRTWNE   **RNSPIG**   **MRSEMU**   **MNAUUT**

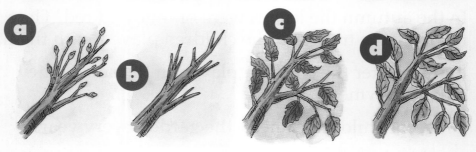

_____   _____   _____   _____

2. Put these sentences in the right order. Write the letters in the boxes.

a) One day, the Giant went to visit his brother.

b) Different children came to the garden every year.

c) Children liked the garden, but the Giant did not like them.

d) A long time ago, a giant lived in a castle with a big garden.

e) Now the children played in the garden every day.

| d | | | | |

After seven years, the Giant came back to his castle. He saw children in his garden. He was very angry. 'Get out of here! It's my garden!' he shouted. 'You can't play here. This garden is MINE!'

'I'm going to build a brick wall,' he said. He built a wall round the garden.

a brick wall

The children were very sad. 'Where can we play?' they said. Sometimes they played in the street, but it was hard and rough. 'The Giant's garden was better than the street,' they said.

The Giant sat in his castle. 'It's nice and quiet now,' he thought. 'It's winter, but soon the spring will come. It will be warm and sunny. The flowers will grow. My garden will be beautiful again.'

But the Spring did not want to come. The Spring said, 'The Giant's too selfish. I like children. I'm not going to go to a sad, empty garden.'

So the Snow, the Wind and the Rain played in the garden. The sun did not shine. Sometimes it was very windy. Sometimes it snowed. Sometimes it rained. It was always cold and grey.

 **Puzzles**

1. Write the right words.

    a) The Giant _____ (see) children in his garden.

    b) The Giant _____ (build) a big brick wall.

    c) The children _____ (be) very sad.

    d) The Giant _____ (sit) in his castle.

    e) The Spring did not come and the garden _____ (be) always cold and grey.

2. What will the weather be? Join the pictures to the right sentences.

    a)   •   • It will rain.

    b)    •   • It will snow.

    c)    •   • It will be sunny.

    d)    •   • It will be cloudy.

    e)    •   • It will be windy.

'Is the spring never going to come?' asked the sad, cold Giant.

Then one day he saw a little bird. 'The bird is singing in my garden!' he said. 'Hooray! The trees and flowers are growing!' He clapped his hands happily.

He looked again. 'The children have made a hole in the wall,' the Giant said. 'They've come back to my garden, and the sun has come with them!'

The Giant was not angry. He was delighted.

delighted

The Giant ran into the garden. He wanted to hug the children, but the children were afraid. They ran away and it became cold again.

'Don't run away,' said the Giant. 'I'm sorry. I was selfish. Please come and play in my garden.'

Only one little boy did not run away. He wanted to climb a tree, but he was too small.

'Don't cry, little boy. I'll help you,' said the Giant. He put the little boy on a branch in the tree. The boy smiled.

'Thank you,' the little boy said.

'You're welcome,' said the Giant.

The boy kissed the Giant's cheek. Spring came into the garden again.

kissed

a cheek

 **Puzzles**

1. How will the story end? Tick one box.

☐   ☐   ☐

2. Find these words in the word square.

wall
welcome
giant
kissed
cheek
delighted
hug
run
afraid
play
bird
selfish
snow

D	B	S	A	X	R	U	N	T
S	E	E	L	B	P	G	N	W
N	A	L	B	M	R	A	X	E
O	A	F	I	P	I	E	G	L
W	C	I	R	G	Y	U	E	C
A	H	S	D	A	H	N	Z	O
C	E	H	L	R	I	T	J	M
M	E	P	W	O	L	D	E	E
W	K	M	K	I	S	S	E	D

The children saw this. They came back into the garden through the hole in the wall.

Now the children played in the garden every day. The Giant played with them. All the children liked the Giant!

But the Giant did not see the little boy again. 'Where's the little boy?' he asked the children, but they did not know.

After ten years, the Giant was old. He did not play now. He looked at his garden and smiled. Many children played in the garden.

Then one day he saw the little boy again. He was under a tree in the garden. The Giant ran out of his castle. He picked up the little boy and kissed him.

The boy said, 'A long time ago you helped me. We are friends. I played in your garden. Now you are going to play in my garden. My garden is Heaven.'

Heaven

In the evening the children came into the garden. They saw the Giant. He was under the same tree. 'Is he asleep?' asked one girl.

'Wake up! Wake up!' said a boy. But the Giant did not wake up.

The Giant was dead. His eyes were closed, but there was a happy smile on his face.

dead

 **Puzzles**

1. Write the right words.

   on   under   into   in   through

   a) The children came _____ the hole.

   b) They came _____ the garden.

   c) They played _____ the garden every day.

   d) The Giant was _____ the tree.

   e) There was a happy smile _____ his face.

2. Who said these? Write the right people.

   a) 'Where's the little boy?'   _____

   b) 'My garden is Heaven.'   _____

   c) 'Is he asleep?'   _____

d) 'Wake up! Wake up!'   _____

Why are the Seasons Different?

This is the Earth. It is on a tilt. It goes round the Sun once a year. This gives us seasons.

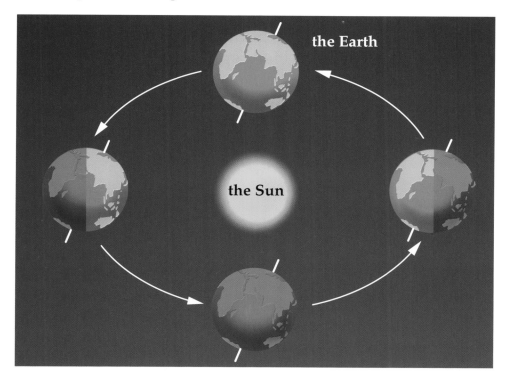

the Earth

the Sun

In the summer, your part of the world is nearer to the Sun. Days are longer. It is warmer. In the winter, your part of the world is further away from the Sun. Days are shorter and nights are longer. It is colder.

a tilt

a part

further

The top half of the Earth is the Northern Hemisphere, and the bottom half of the Earth is the Southern Hemisphere.

The Equator is the line round the middle of the Earth. It is always hot at places on the Equator.

When it is summer in the Southern Hemisphere, it is winter in the Northern Hemisphere.

Northern Hemisphere

the Equator

Southern Hemisphere

 **Puzzles**

1. Read the sentences. Write the right words.

   a) The Earth goes round this.

   b) Your part of the world is nearer the Sun in this season.

   c) Days are shorter in this season.

   d) In the summer, days are _____.

   e) This is the line round the middle of the Earth.

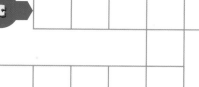

2. Write these words in the right order. Make sentences.

   a) once / the / round / Earth / year / a / goes / Sun / the.

   _____

   b) Hemisphere / the / half / is / top / the / of / Earth / the / Northern.

   _____ 19

Japan is in the Northern Hemisphere. Spring is from March to May in Japan. In the spring, people wait to see the flowers on the cherry blossom trees. Then they have parties under the trees. This is the *Hanami* Festival.

JAPAN

cherry blossom trees

The longest day in the Northern Hemisphere is on 21 or 22 June each year. This is the middle of summer. There is a flower festival for four days each June in California, USA. There is a parade and people go to flower fields to look at the flowers.

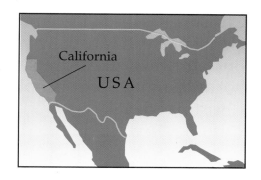

There is a Chinese festival in the autumn. It is the Mid-Autumn Festival. People wait to see a big round moon in the night sky. They eat mooncakes and they light lanterns.

a parade

fields

mooncakes

lanterns

Christmas is on 25 December. It is winter in the Northern Hemisphere. It is usually very cold. Sometimes it snows. But Christmas in Australia is in the summer. It is usually hot and sunny. Some people go to the beach on Christmas day!

AUSTRALIA

Puzzles

Write the right words.
a) People have parties at the *Hanami* Festival in
   _____.

b) There is a flower festival in the summer in
   _____, USA.

c) At Mid-Autumn Festival people eat _____.

d) Some people go to the beach at Christmas in
   _____.

Questions

Page 1   a) What was in the Giant's garden?
         b) Was the Giant selfish?

Page 2   a) What did the children do in the river?
         b) What did the children chase?

Page 3   *True* or *false*?
         a) In the summer the children rolled on the leaves.
         b) In the winter the children made snowmen.

Page 5   a) 'This garden is _____!' the Giant shouted.
         b) The Giant built a _____ round the garden.

Page 6   a) Were the children happy?
         b) Where did the children play?

Page 7   a) The Spring did not want to come to an **selfish** / **empty** / **cold** garden.
         b) The Giant's garden was **green** / **grey** / **blue**.

Page 9   a) What did the Giant see one day?
         b) What did the children make in the wall?

Page 10 *True* or *false*?
         a) The Giant wanted to hug the children.
         b) Only two little boys did not run away.

Page 11 a) The Giant put the little boy on a _____
in the tree.
b) The boy _____ the Giant's cheek.

Page 13 a) Who came back into the garden?
b) Who played with the children?

Page 14 a) After ten years, the Giant was
happy / sad / old.
b) The little boy was **under / in / on** a tree.

Page 15 a) Was the Giant asleep?
b) What was on the Giant's face?

Page 17 *True* or *false*?
a) The Sun goes round the Earth.
b) In the winter, days are shorter.

Page 18 a) The **top / bottom** half of the Earth is the
Southern Hemisphere.
b) It is always **cold / hot** at places on the
Equator.

Page 20 a) Where do people have parties in Japan?
b) What season is the *Hanami* Festival in?

Page 21 a) There is a _____ festival each June in
California, USA.
b) There is a Chinese festival in the
_____.

Page 22 a) When is Christmas?
b) In Australia, where do some people go on
Christmas day?